SPIRIT OF DANCE
THE NEXT STEPS

Anna Barton

Findhorn Press

ISBN 0 905249 82 8
First published 1992
Design & layout by Claudia Klingemann, Bay Area Graphics
Cover painting © Lawry Gold
Music notation by Barbara Swetina and Chris Power
Lyric notation and translation by Kate Holly O'Connell and Anna Barton
Dance instructions by Anna Barton
Printed and bound by Posthouse Printing, Whitemire, Moray

Published by Findhorn Press, The Park, Findhorn,
Forres IV36 0TZ, Scotland

CONTENTS

The steps and information in this booklet are correct to the best of my knowledge.

It is possible to learn the basic steps and movements of the dances on the *Spirit of Dance: The Next Steps* cassette using this booklet. However, the instructions are only simple, and to learn the individual style and little nuances of each dance you should try to join a dance group. For information on such groups, see the 'Grapevine' Sacred/Circle Dance newsletter (contact Judy King, 75 Newtown Road, Eastleigh, Hants SO5 4BX).

See the end of this book for information on ordering audio cassettes, video cassettes and booklets.

INTRODUCTION

When Professor Bernhard Wosien visited the Findhorn Community and gave us our first dozen dances in a workshop back in 1976, I never dreamed how much Sacred Dance, also known as Circle Dance, would expand and bring joy and hope to so many people on the planet. The dances he brought us, together with some that we have collected ourselves and others that have been created in the last few years, add up to Sacred Dance as it is today. It is a magnificent tool for helping us recognise ourselves as part of the whole. By dancing together we bring healing to ourselves and our planet, and discover that it is possible to do the same thing in our everyday lives.

These dances have evolved gradually and there are many other variations which you may meet. We try to preserve the authentic steps as far as possible (although what is 'authentic' when the same dance varies from village to village?) but we do not claim to be folk dance experts. We do know, however, that by dancing in these circles we can improve and enrich our lives physically, mentally, emotionally and spiritually and this rubs off on everyone with whom we come into contact. We learn to communicate in a deeper and more meaningful way which eventually can only help to improve and enrich the whole world.

It is with great pleasure that we now offer you our second Sacred Dance collection, *Spirit of Dance: The Next Steps*, in the form of this booklet and audio and video cassettes. We hope that you will enjoy dancing and listening to them as much as we have enjoyed making them.

Anna Barton

R	—	right foot
L	—	left foot
s	—	side
b	—	back or behind
xb	—	cross behind
f	—	front or forward
xf	—	cross forward
cl.	—	close
h	—	hop
k	—	kick
pf	—	point forward
ps	—	point side
pb	—	point back (behind)
flex	—	bend and straighten knees in one beat
repl.	—	replace
st.	—	stamp
V	—	man
U	—	woman
cw	—	clockwise
a/cw	—	anti-clockwise
l	—	lift

— —	—	one beat
= —	—	two beats
ꞈ	—	half beat
⟶		direction of dance
↑		towards the centre
↪		turn to face other direction
↻		turn on the spot
∩		position of dancer (facing centre)
⟶∩⟶		moving R facing centre
⟹		moving R facing R
𝄞		'V' hand-hold
		'W' hand-hold

'Pas de bas' or 'Pas de basque'

R	L	R	L	R	L
ꞈ	ꞈ		ꞈ	ꞈ	
s	cl.	repl.	s	cl.	repl.

Kos Greeting Dance (Ena Mythos)

Greece

Circle. Hands joined with arms crossed right over left.

Music by M. Hadjidakis. Words by the poet V. Rotas for the performance of Aristophanes' comedy *The Birds*, in a free translation of the ancient Greek text.

This was possibly danced on the Greek Island of Cos by fishermen's families to welcome them safely home. The Knights Templar danced it during the Crusades. The crossed arms symbolise the spiral, which denotes strength, unity and eternity. They also represent the cross of St Andrew.

Kos is spelt with a 'K' because Bernhard Wosien named this dance and spelt it the German way.

1 [Ena mytho tha sas poh
Puh tou mathameh pediah] x2
Itan kapios mia fora
Pu fighe stinerimia
2 [ki apo tote sta vouna
zouse pia me to kinighi] x2
kiapo misos stis ghinekes
then katevi sta choria.

3 [Ghia tou mytho pou mas lete
allo mytho tha sas po] x2
Itan kapios mia fora
dhichos spiti ke ghonia
4 [Ghia tous andres iche frichi
ki ena misos floghero] x2
omos oles tis ghinekes
tis agapaye tharo.

I'm going to tell you a story that we learned as children.
There was once a man who left the desert and lived from hunting.
He didn't go down to the village because he hated women.
For the story you tell, I'll tell another.
There was someone without any home.
He had a strong horror and hate of men, but he loved women.

Hands joined with arms crossed right over left

I greet you			I give you space and I take my space			I move on		
L	R	L R	R	L	L R	R	L	L R
f	cl.	flex	b	cl.	flex	s	cl.	flex
	+ flex	knees		+ flex			+ flex	
	knees							

Ajde Jano

Yugoslavia (Serbia)
Circle. 'V' hand-hold.

Dance choreographed by Anatol Jankowski (a ballet dancer) in the USA.
Music traditional.

Ajde Jano kolo da igramo
Ajde Jano Ajde Dušo kolo da igramo

Ajde Jano konja da prodamo
Ajde Jano Ajde Dušo konja da prodamo

Ajde Jano kuču da prodamo
Ajde Jano Ajde Dušo kuču da prodamo

Da prodamo samo da igramo
Da prodamo Jano Dušo samo da igramo

Come Jano, let's dance the kolo.
Sell the horse, sell the house, sell everything, just dance.

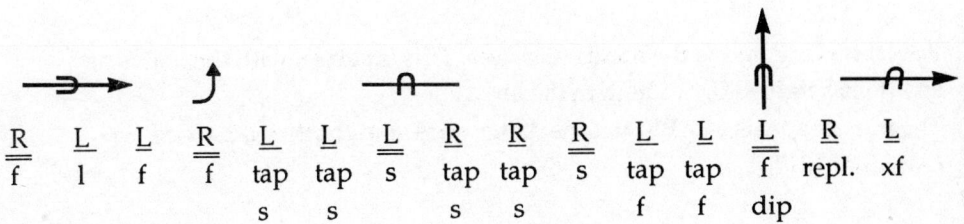

9

Ambi Dagets

Armenia
Circle or line. 'W' hand-hold, holding little fingers.

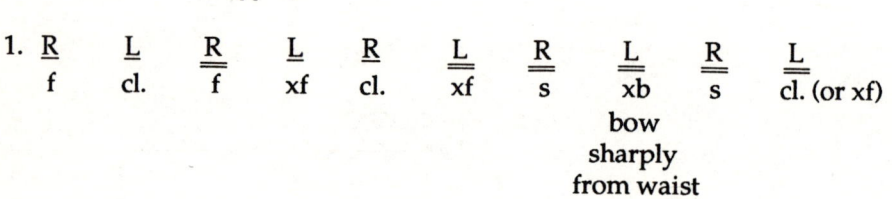

1.	R	L	R	L	R	L	R	L	R	L
	f	cl.	f	xf	cl.	xf	s	xb	s	cl. (or xf)

bow
sharply
from waist

2.	R	L	R	L		L	R	L	R
	turn	to	right	lift		turn	to	left	lift
				or point					or point

Whilst turning, move the hands in circles. This is subtle, with the hands at shoulder height still, not high in the air.
The music repeats (AABB) but the dance goes straight through twice (ABAB or 1212)

Nigun Shel Yossi

Israel

Yossi's (or Joseph's) tune

Couples dance in circle, man on left of partner. 'V' hand-hold.

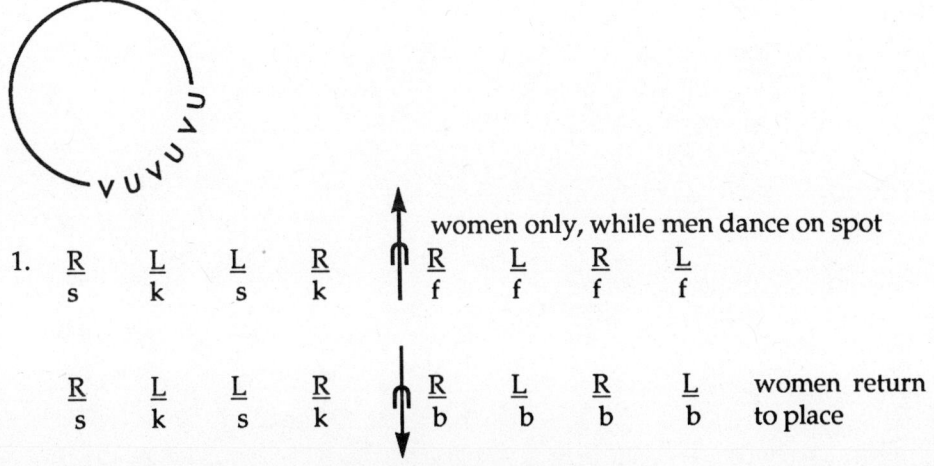

					women only, while men dance on spot			
1.	R	L	L	R	R	L	R	L
	s	k	s	k	f	f	f	f

	R	L	L	R	R	L	R	L	women return
	s	k	s	k	b	b	b	b	to place

2. Part 1 is repeated with men going in and out.

3. Facing partners:

Snap fingers R & L when you step $\underset{s}{\underline{\underline{R}}}$ $\underset{s}{\underline{\underline{L}}}$

Pass partner with 4 steps, woman on outside of the circle. Meeting next partner, R hands around waists, L hand held in the air, turn 8 steps with emphasis on the odd numbers. When back in place, repeat whole of part 3, making sure you are ready to start from the beginning again.

I learnt this dance originally with everyone going in and out together in parts 1 and 2, but as we always seemed to crash into each other I suggested we take turns. We have done it this way ever since.

Misirlou (Tango)

Greek/American
Circle. 'W' hand-hold.

I discovered during a workshop in Athens that Misirlou means 'Egyptian girl', and the song in this tango form was originally used by a woman in America to accompany a variation of Surtos Kritikos, as she didn't have any Greek music. The dance became very popular under the title Misirlou. In later years Theodorakis composed a tune to the poem *Eleftheria* (freedom) by G. Seferis and this music has become known in dance circles as Misirlou. The Greek people object to this, as the original Misirlou music is used in bars and cabaret and is associated with belly dancing and alcohol, whereas Theodorakis is a very well-respected composer.

Misirlou mou ee yleekya sou ee matya
Floya m'ehee anapsee mesa steen karthya
Ah ya chabibi ah ya lelelee ah
Ta thyo sou heelee stazoune melee oyme

Ach Misirlou
Trella tha mou erthee then eepofero pya
Ah tha se klepso mesa apo teen arapya

Mavromata Misirlou mou trellee
Ee zoee mou alazee mesa sto feelee
Ah ya chabibi ah ya lelelee ah
Ap to theeko sou to stomataki oyme

My Misirlou, your sweet glance
Has lit a fire within my heart
O woe is me
Your two lips drip honey

O Misirlou,
Madness has seized me, I can bear it no more
I'm going to kidnap you so we can elope

My Misirlou, brown-eyed and crazy
My life is changing when we kiss
O woe is me
My life is changing when I kiss your sweet mouth

'W' hand-hold

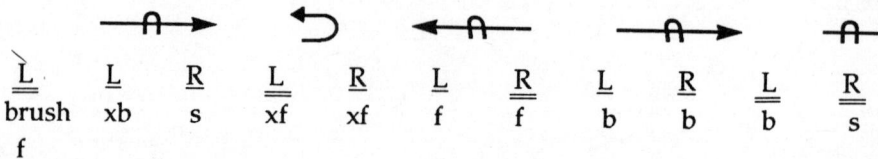

L	L	R	L	R	L	R	L	R	L	R
brush	xb	s	xf	xf	f	f	b	b	b	s
f										

Variations:

1.

L	L	R	L	R	L	R	L	R	L	R
brush	xb	s	xf	xf	f	f	xf	f	f	s
f										

2.

L	L	R	L	R	L	R	L	R	L	R
brush	xb	s	xf	xf	s	xb	repl.	s	xb	s
f										

Lompka po Lompka

Yugoslavia
Circle. 'V' hand-hold.

'V' hand-hold

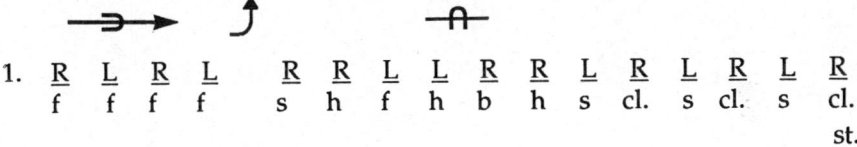

1. R L R L   R R L L R R L R L R L R
   f f f f   s h f h b h s cl. s cl. s cl.
                                          st.

When the music changes key after 12 sequences, change to part 2 by taking 8 steps forward, then start part 2.

2. R R L L R R L L   R R L L R R [L R] x 4 L R
   f h f h f h f h   s h f h b h [s cl.]   s cl.
                                                   st.

Adjon az Isten

Hungary
Circle. 'V' hand-hold.

There are several versions of this dance going around the circle dance network, but I prefer this version which I learnt from Laura Shannon.

The song is sung in Budapest Hungarian—not an old dialect. The band that plays the original is known for its creative music and arrangements and this tune is not a traditional Hungarian one.

Adjon az isten szerencse't
Szerelmet, forro' kemence't
Ūres vika'mban gabona't.
Àrva kezemben parolàt.

Làmpàmban làngot, ne kejjen
Koràn az àgyra hevernem.
Kèrdèsre vàlaszt ō kūldjōn.
Hogy hitem szèljen ne dūljōn.

Adjon az isten fènyeket
Temetōk helyet életet.
Nekem a kèrés nagy szégyen.
Adjon ùgy is ha nem kérem.

God gives me a roof over my head, food on my table and a fire in my hearth. I ask these things of him, but he would give them to me even if I didn't ask.

'V' hand-hold

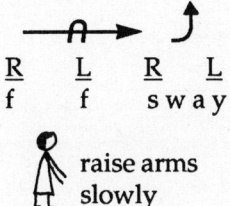

R	L	R	L
f	f	s w a y	

raise arms
slowly

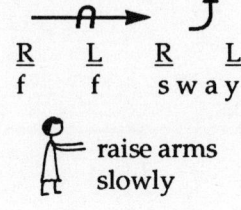

R	L	R	L
f	f	s w a y	

raise arms
slowly

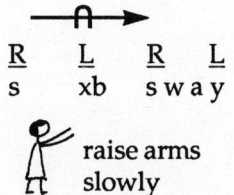

R	L	R	L
s	xb	s w a y	

raise arms
slowly

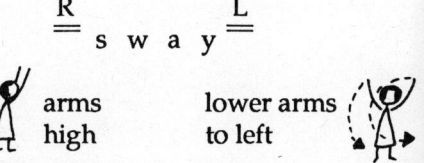

R
= s w a y = L

arms   lower arms
high   to left

L'Allouette

France
Circle. 'V' hand-hold.

This is a branle, danced all over France and possibly dating back to the Middle Ages. It is danced in a closed circle or in a snake that weaves around.

1. [L   R   L   R] x 2   2. [L   R   L   R   L   R] x 2
    s · cl. s   cl.   s   cl. s   s   cl.   s

Arms swing loosely forward and back in time to the music.

1. L'Allouette sur la branche x 2
   Chorus
   Faites un petit saut, l'allouette, l'allouette.
   Faites un petit saut, l'allouette, comme il faut.

2. Mettez vos bras en liance x 2
   Chorus

3. Faites nous trois pas de danse x 2
   Chorus

4. Faites nous la réverance x 2
   Chorus

Chekassia Kfula

Israel

Circle. 'V' hand-hold or back basket weave, L arm on top.

1. $\begin{bmatrix} \begin{array}{cccc} \text{R} & \text{L} & \text{R} & \text{L} \\ \text{xf} & \text{s} & \text{xb} & \text{s} \end{array} \end{bmatrix}$ x 3 $\quad \begin{array}{cccc} \text{R} & \text{L} & \text{R} & \text{L} \quad \text{(rock)} \\ \text{xf} & \text{repl.} & \text{xf} & \text{repl.} \end{array}$ x 2

2. $\begin{bmatrix} \begin{array}{cccccc} \text{R} & \text{L} & \text{R} & \text{L} & \text{R} & \text{L} \\ \text{xf} & \text{repl.} & \text{s} & \text{xf} & \text{repl.} & \text{s} \end{array}$ x 2 $\quad \begin{array}{cccc} \text{R} & \text{L} & \text{R} & \text{L} \\ \text{xf} & \text{repl.} & \text{xf} & \text{repl.} \end{array} \end{bmatrix}$ x 2

Traditionally a couples' dance with skaters' hold.

Ssulum Ja'Akov (Jacob's Ladder)

Israel

Circle. 'V' hand-hold.

Represents Jacob's dream with the angels walking up and down the ladder.

'V' hand-hold

1.

[
R	L	R	L	R		L	R	L	R	L
s	cl.	s	f	f		s	cl.	s	b	b
] x 2

2.

[
R	L	L	R	L	R	L	R	L	R	L
s	pf	xb	s	xf	xf	s	xb	repl.	s	xb
] x 2

The rhythm changes but the steps remain the same.

Irish Mandala

Brian Boru's March

I learnt the Irish Mandala in Paris and later on, reading the cover of a Scottish dance record, I discovered the same steps as a variation of the Gay Gordons.

A couples' dance in a circle with the man on the inside. Start in an anti-clockwise direction.

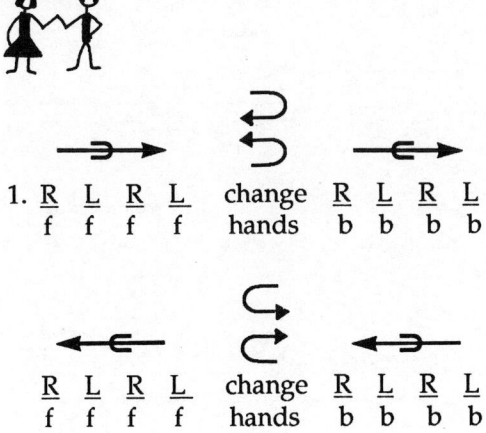

1. R L R L   change   R L R L
   f f f f   hands   b b b b

   R L R L   change   R L R L
   f f f f   hands   b b b b

2. 'Pas de basque' towards each other and away from each other. Man moves to woman's place in 4 steps, woman turns around man, facing him into his place, changing hands, in 4 steps.

3. Repeat the two 'pas de basque', man walks forward 4 steps diagonally to meet new partner. Woman turns right under man's arm (facing him) and back diagonally in 4 steps to meet new partner.

Chiotikos

Chios, Greece
Circle. 'W' hand-hold.

'W' hand-hold

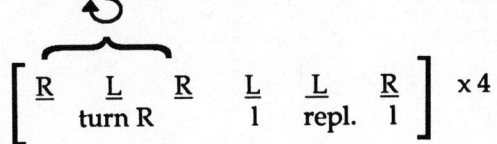

1. $\left[\begin{array}{cccccc} R & L & R & L & L & R \\ f & f & f & l & s & l \end{array}\right]$ x 4

2. Drop hands

$\left[\begin{array}{cccccc} R & L & R & L & L & R \\ & \text{turn R} & & l & \text{repl.} & l \end{array}\right]$ x 4

3. $\left[\begin{array}{cccccccc} R & L & R & L & L & R & L & R \\ s & xb & s & l & s & xb & s & l \end{array}\right]$ x 2

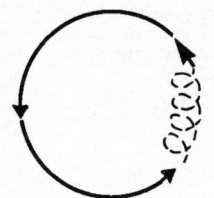

Can be danced in a 'horseshoe', where in part 2 the leader dances across the gap to be the last person.

The musical 'introduction' before the start of the dance is also the music for part 3.

Healing and Wholeness

Joc de Leagane—a Romanian lullaby
A very slow meditation dance in a circle. 'V' hand-hold.

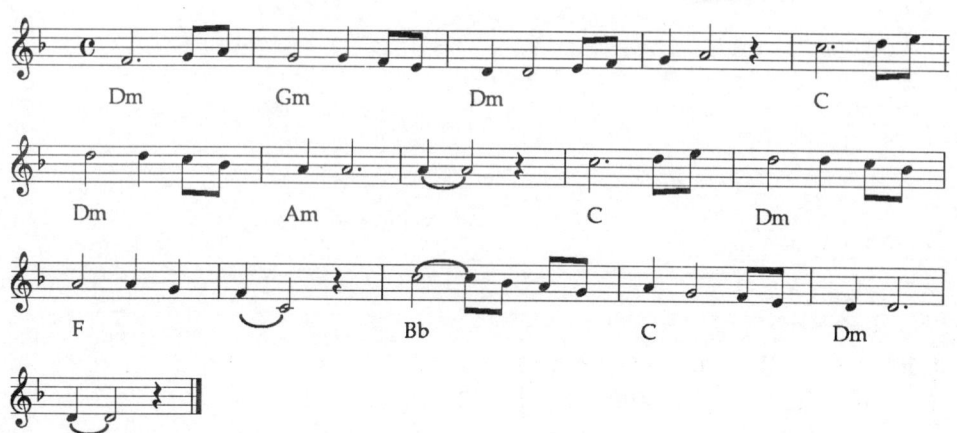

'Joc', meaning 'dance', was not part of the original title. Traditionally it would not have been sung in parts. Village songs were sung in unison or with drones. The parts are from a modern composer.

I choreographed this dance several years ago with John Ralph. The steps and movements came very naturally to us and a long time later I realised their significance.

Mama cînd mo leganat
Numai de dor mio cîntat

Mio cîntat de dor sio plins
Dorul de mine so prins

De cînd port dor la inima
Numai am nici o hodina
Nici la prinz si nici la cină

Cite doruri reles grele
Tates pa bra tele mele

Altul moare de batrîn
Nu sti dorul de cei bun

Dar eu stiu ca lam purtat
De cînd mama mio cîntat

Lai, lai, lai etc.

When my mother cradled me in her arms, she sang to me only of love. And so many times she sang to me that I have never known hatred. How painful have been the times when my love has not been returned. Anyone who dies of old age cannot know the truth of love. But I know the truth. I feel it deep in my heart because my mother gave it to me.

'V' hand-hold. A very slow meditation dance — one step every two beats.

1.

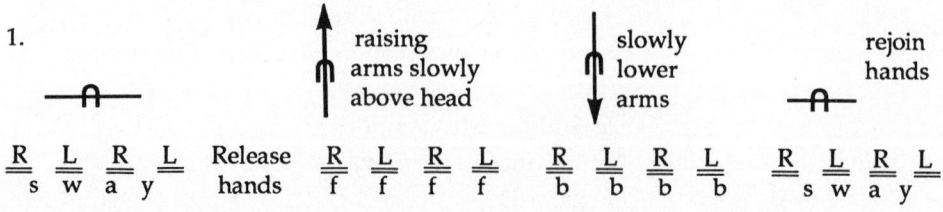

R	L	R	L	Release	R	L	R	L		R	L	R	L		R	L	R	L
s	w	a	y	hands	f	f	f	f		b	b	b	b		s	w	a	y

Individually we seek and find the Spirit.

2.

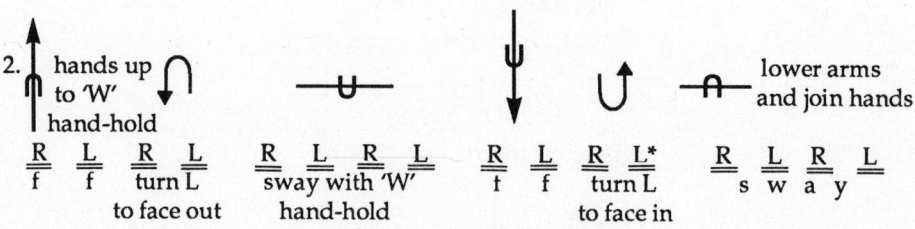

R	L	R	L		R	L	R	L		R	L	R	L*		R	L	R	L
f	f	turn L			sway with 'W'					t	f	turn L			s	w	a	y
		to face out			hand-hold							to face in						

* Raise eyes and 'give thanks' with hands palms up in 'W'.

Having discovered Spirit individually we turn outwards and find we are not alone.

3.

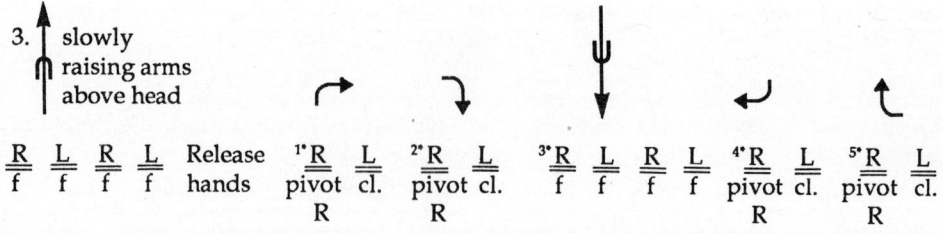

R	L	R	L	Release	¹ʳR	L	²ⁿR	L	³ʳR	L	R	L	⁴ᵗR	L	⁵ᵗR	L
f	f	f	f	hands	pivot	cl.	pivot	cl.	f	f	f	f	pivot	cl.	pivot	cl.
					R		R						R		R	

1*   Lower R arm to shoulder level keeping it straight, palm up, following it
        with the eyes.

2*   Lower L arm completely to inside of circle and sweep up and out in front
        of you to join R arm, palm up.

3*   'Giving' gesture with hands as you walk forward.

4*   Touch finger tips of R and L hands, forming a circle with arms.

5*   Draw hands towards you and cross them on your chest.

We open ourselves to Spirit, drawing down the energy (R hand), and gather up Earth
energy (L hand), then we give it out to the world. Having given all, we nourish ourselves
by closing and going inwards.

Repeat parts 1, 2 and 3. Repeat part 1 leaving hands joined all the time.

The tape that accompanies this book is the result of the enthusiasm we have for creating live music for groups to dance to. We have given the music complex arrangements so that it will be a rich listening experience while keeping the spirit of live performance throughout. We have included as much of the music and words in this booklet as possible to enable you to re-create the experience yourselves if you can. I highly recommend live music—even if it is not to a professional standard—for its rapport with and immediacy for the dancers.

We have worked to convey the flavour of the original songs as closely as possible. We realise, however, that creating an authentic Greek, Hungarian, Israeli or Armenian atmosphere is beyond our scope. In turn we offer our own ideas and enthusiasm to create something of our own of these songs and tunes. We hope our efforts will affect you with excitement and fun, with soul and feeling. We have done our best to be true to the 'spirit' of the dance and trust that in listening and dancing you will experience the same.

Yours in truth,
Rory O'Connell

ORDERING INFORMATION

Spirit of Dance: The Next Steps, by the Findhorn Sacred Dance Band, is the music cassette that accompanies this booklet. It costs £7.45 plus postage and packing. For details of how to order this cassette and copies of this booklet, please contact Findhorn Press, The Park, Findhorn, Forres IV36 0TZ, Scotland or telephone (0309) 690582.

A video cassette showing the dances in detail will be available by spring 1992. Please contact Findhorn Press for details.